A Collector's Guide to
Salem Witchcraft & Souvenirs

Pamela Apkarian-Russell

PHOTOGRAPHY BY CHRISTOPHER J. RUSSELL

Schiffer Publishing Ltd

4880 Lower Valley Road, Atglen, PA 19310 USA

DEDICATION

This book is dedicated to the memory of the Salem Witches, who lost their lives, properties, dignity, and freedom during the 1691 reign of terror. The names of those who died will live on in history books, but those like the children of the Reverend George Burroughs, who were turned out of their home in the dead of winter by their stepmother, were also victims and suffered as much from the hysteria as those accused of witchcraft. The injustice touched everyone, though, including the survivors. Therefore this book is dedicated to all holocaust survivors of every race, creed, and nationality, especially the forgotten survivors of the Armenian Holocaust, like my father Apkar Apkarian, and my grandparents Yathazar and Noonia Simonian. It is to the survivors of all injustices this book is dedicated.

Copyright © 1998 by Pamela Apkarian-Russell
Library of Congress Catalog Card Number: 97-80136

Book Design by: Laurie A. Smucker

ISBN: 0-7643-0425-9
Printed in China

Published by Schiffer Publishing Ltd.
4880 Lower Valley Road
Atglen, Pa 19310
Phone: (610) 593-1777 ; Fax: (610) 593-2002
Email: Schiffferbk@aol.com
Please write for a free catalog.
This book may be purchased from the publisher.
Please include $3.95 for shipping.

Please try your bookstore first.

ACKNOWLEDGEMENTS

I would like to thank all those who have aided and abetted me with this book, especially Sue Erickson, who for years has haunted me with "When are you going to do a book on Salem Witch collectables?" Though I have heard this from many subscribers to the *Trick or Treat Trader*, she has been the most enthusiastic and persistent. I would like to thank Michael Michaud, Susan Erickson, Connie Halket, and Debbie Dwyer for lending us items to photograph from their collections. I also, want to thank all those people who asked us not to forget the social significance of the subject: the plight of those whose voices were not heard until it was to late. I hope I have not disappointed those social historians. A special thanks to Kathy Bowen for being only a phone call away when I needed to bemoan my computer illiteracy problems. I can not thank Peter Schiffer and Douglas Congdon-Martin of Schiffer Publishing enough for extricating me from those computer problems, which were many and exasperating for both them and me. Without the help and good will of all of these wonderful people, this book would not be possible.

Pamela E. Apkarian-Russell

Contents

A WORD ON PRICING

Prices on Salem Witch items fluctuate according to the type of collector who is buying. As many pieces fall into more than one collecting sphere, it is quite probable that one group will value an item higher than another. For instance, sewing collectors will pay more for a thimble than the general Salem Witch collector. I have tried to set a fair, average price that a collector would pay for an item if they didn't own it already. This is a guide with suggested values, not rigid, inflexible facts. As most of the items in this book are from my personal collection, I hope no one will presume they are for sale—they are not. If anything, I am always pursuing items for my collection, and for resale. The price of any item should be based on how much you like a piece and what you are prepared to pay to own that item. An item might be listed at two hundred dollars, but if it isn't an item that calls out to you and says "Take me home," then you might only be willing to pay fifty dollars for it. Then again, if that item is your heart's desire and you just won the lottery, you'll be happy to pay the going price. The beauty of collecting is the fun of the chase and the joy of owning an item that is beautiful, interesting, or intriguing. Enjoy these items. And, remember, a fair price is always the best price. We hope this book will whet your appetite for pursuing the historic facts behind the Salem witch trials, as well as the collectibles. Happy hunting.

— Pamela E. Apkarian-Russell

Introduction

The Salem Witch trials were the result of a religious intolerance brought to this country by the pilgrims. Any aberration from set church rule, be it religious or social, was punishable. The "witches of Salem" were not the first innocents to loose their lives in America. What made this episode stand out in history was not only the number of people who lost their lives but the surprising number of socially prominent people who were movers in the trials, and who stood to profit economically and socially, like Cotton Mather, who dreamed of becoming president of Harvard College. He and the Reverend Samuel Parris and Thomas Putnam were the three major moving forces of the trials.

There are many theories about what sparked the complaints and ensuing accusations of the "bewitched girls." Many theories and so little proof. One theory was that, as was custom in the day, the women made rope of hemp (or marijuana), chewing it to make it pliable, hence the hallucinations. Another was that these manifestations may have been induced by fear, hypnotism, and mass hysteria. Whatever the theory, the fact is that the symptoms the girls suffered were real. The truth can never be known, so the controversy goes on and interest grows. Speculation is a heady fruit, but facts are a more substantial meal.

The two-volume book published in 1867 by Charles Upham, *Salem Witchcraft,* is by far the most scholarly book written on the trials, the circumstances leading up to them, and the aftermath. As with most catastrophes of social importance, they were part and parcel of the social mores of the times. There is an evolutionary process for social and economic change, whether that change be good or bad. Suffrage could not have been accomplished during the Civil War, nor could people have marched for civil rights in the 1920s. The trials are an important part of American judicial and social history, and even have global importance since Massachusetts Governor Sir William Phips suspended the trials until word could be brought from Queen Anne about how to proceed. The greatest impact, however, was locally—many Salem-area families suffered from the turmoil and havoc.

Salem is very much the typical coastal tourist town today, and has been for over a century. In 1898, a department store in Salem, Daniel Low, had a spoon made to sell to the many tourists that were drawn to the town by the story of the witch trials. The fairly plain design was so enthusiastically received that a second design, much more elaborate than the first, was added to the store's inventory.

From spoons it was just a matter of time before the repertoire was expanded to include many other items that portrayed witches. Almost overnight the spoon collecting rage was born and souvenir china mania was standing in line waiting for a chance to explode on a society that was, with the invention of the car and buses, becoming more and more mobile. Daniel Low had given birth to the souvenir collecting craze. It was only a short time before other companies followed suit and other towns rushed to put their historic sites on pieces of china and silver.

Daniel Low the department store, a landmark in Salem for over one hundred years, recently closed its doors forever, but the statement it made on quality and the impact it had on collectibles is ongoing. Other stores in Salem sold souvenirs and local companies produced items like soda or milk with the witch as their logo. The Salem police department has a wonderful shirt patch incorporating the witch logo. The witch has become the symbol of Salem, a symbol that frightened the inhabitants of the same town three hundred years before.

One can not separate the souvenir trade from the historic trials. Without the one the other could not have happened. The average tourist in the years proceeding 1898 wanted to see where these historic events took place and to purchase a small souvenir of their visit. Photography was just coming into the everyday lives of the average American and picture postcards were a very important part of communication with friends and families. A day trip from Boston or Worcester on the train was a big deal for many who were eager to see the sights and bring home a small momento to show to friends and family.

Today, we still send picture postcards from the places we visit and we still bring back momentos to make us feel nostalgic about those places. Salem was, at the turn of the century, like going to Disneyland. It was like walking into a history book and seeing the actual places—Gallows Hills, the Witch House, the homes of Rebecca Nourse and the Putnams, and where the jail would have stood.

The history of Salem is full of ghosts and the images of suffering, injustice, cruelty, man's inhumanity to man, hysteria, greed, and of fear born of ignorance. The accusers faced the noble and dignified sufferings of the unjustly accused, like Rebecca Nourse, the elderly invalid who was educated beyond many of her neighbors and defended herself with quiet dignity. She—along with those who lost their lives, dignity, honor, and property—were victims of their time.

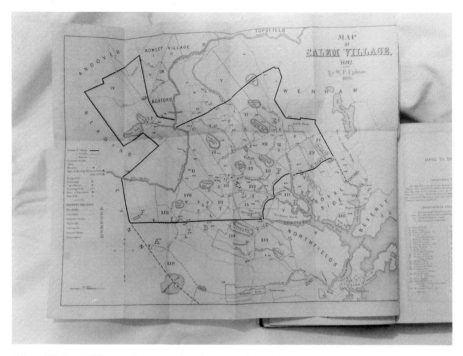

Map of Salem Village as it was during the days of the trials. This is from the Charles Upham book, *Salem Witchcraft*, and shows the different plots of land belonging to the different families. Upham's book remains, after all these years, the premier study on the trials. Two-volume book with map still attached, $125.

The police department of Salem sells these cloth patches for $5 each. A bewitching bargain to say the least. *From the Susan Erickson collection.*

PART 1
𝕳istory

The year is 1691, the place Salem, Massachusetts, and you are being accused of witchcraft. The penalty is death by hanging. You are an old woman, ill and poor—the court will not allow you a lawyer. The witnesses against you are your neighbors, children, husband, former friends, a group of hysterical teenage girls, and ghosts. You are innocent but you can't prove it. According to the law you are guilty until proven innocent. What can you do?

It is now over two hundred years later, nearly the end of the nineteen century, and you are in the same city buying postcards of the house where it all took place. Collectibles are sold to tourists and residents alike in this historic seaport town of myth, magic, and witchcraft. You have gone to all the historic sites, read the guidebooks, and it all seems so familiar.

Jump to the current decade, to an antique show where you find a sterling silver thimble with a witch motif from Salem, Massachusetts. It looks so familiar. Is it deja vu? Is it witchcraft?

Whatever the cause, a mysterious sense of connectedness to this American tragedy that took place nearly three hundred years ago makes the trinkets and witch-motif souvenirs from the seaside city of Salem as bewitching today as they were one hundred years ago.

As any spoon collector can attest, the souvenir trade began in historic Salem. The name Daniel Low will live on as the innovator that sparked the souvenir craze in this country. Thinking to intrigue the many tourists who flocked to Salem, the company made its first souvenir, a spoon. Its success was so pronounced that a second spoon soon followed suit.

The first design was of a witch complete with broom, the word "Salem" in large letters, and three pins that were supposedly used to bewitch victims. "D. Low Sterling" and a symbol of a circled D (for Durgin silversmiths) is the mark one will find on the back of the first Salem Witch spoon.

Durgin Silversmiths were later bought out by Gorham Silversmiths. The first Salem witch spoon was patented on March 3, 1891, according to Low. However, no such patent was found listed with the patent office. The trademark of the witch, however, was patented on January 13, 1891, patent number 18,838.

The number one design is plain in comparison to a second design, made by Gorham manufacturing and marked with a "G," an anchor, and a lion on the back of the bowl in a pseudo hallmark. The second design has more detail and

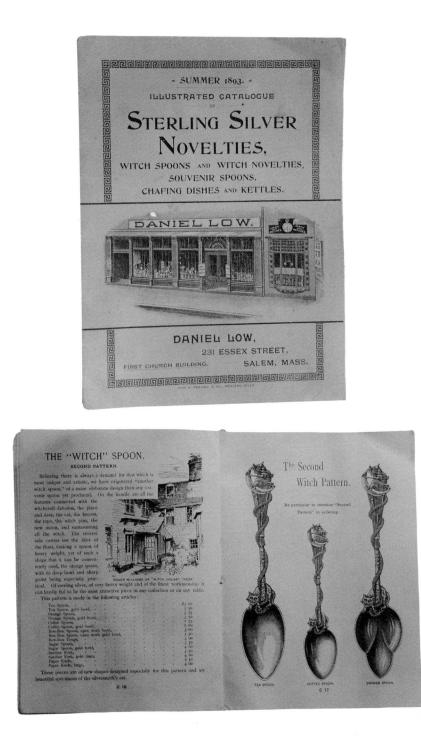

Front and back cover of the Daniel Low catalog for 1893. *From the collection of Connie Halket.*

The Witch House, where the infamous trials took place, is Salem's most visited site, and the most photographed house since the invention of the camera.

The Salem witch trade is thriving, with lots of modern items in production. The Witch Museum is one of many places where modern souvenirs may be purchased. Cup and saucer $12; pennant, $5.

ornamentation. It is die cut and shows a witch on a crescent moon at the top of the spoon, with a cat extended from the bowl. The three pins used as evidence in the trials and the date of 1692 are on the handle and are integrated with a twining hemp rope, all against the handle of a witch's broom. The design twines around the back of the spoon showing the back of the witch, cat, and broom, again with the rope twisting about but showing the end, which was frayed and cut. The multidimensional effect, the historic symbols, and the finality of the hangman's rope, make it a beautifully designed spoon. It is not surprising that they sold so well to an eager public that clamored for more.

The building which Daniel Low occupied for well over one hundred years stands at 231 Essex Street in Salem. Unfortunately, the company recently closed its doors.

Low then began a line of items for the Witch City trade that would be imitated by towns and cities across the United States, Canada, Europe, and, indeed, in tourist havens around the world. Other merchants in Salem commissioned items to be sold exclusively in their stores. Sterling items were the high-caliber items that Low began with, but soon the public was insisting on more items at a moderate price. The market escalated and soon items were being made of china, glass, plate, pottery, and celluloid.

The city itself used the witch motif as its emblem or logo, so it was only to be expected that dairies and soda companies would put the witch on their bottles, that witch hazel, which was very popular at the turn of the century, would use the witch logo, and that every store or company that was in the area and could claim historic affiliation, or incorporate it into usage, did so.

The souvenir trade was born and blossomed in Salem and, like the witch trials themselves, fascinated people to the point that a crazed frenzy of collecting began. Today these items, be they spoons, plates, dishes, thimbles, etc., are still collected. Their beauty, historic interest, and decorative possibilities have continued to charm people for more than a hundred years following their first appearance on the market. The collectibles that have been produced for the Salem witch trade are not copies of actual items used in the trials, nor are they gruesome reminders of a dark remnant of our nation's history. They are stylized witches that represent the past of a city rather than the residents who lived or died during that reign of terror.

It is almost amusing to wonder what Cotton Mather's reaction would have been had he known his actions would be held against him and that the witches he hated so venomously would become the symbol of the town. It is comforting to know that, in the end, the three men who most influenced those trials not only did not achieve their objectives, but lost those things that were most dear to their hearts and egos.

Interest in Salem witch collectibles derives from a combination of historic interest, interest in the occult, and antique appreciation. Many things have combined to keep that interest alive. Arthur Miller's play *The Crucible* is a work of art that has spurred more interest in this segment of American history. The fact that the play has recently been made into a movie will introduce many more people to the Salem trials. Our school history books only give a smidgen of thought to the trials, yet what happened three hundred years ago has influenced our judicial system and our government. "Innocent until proven guilty," "no spectral evidence," "no hearsay," "freedom of religion," and many other related issues were taken into deep consideration by the founding fathers, especially Thomas Jefferson, who helped shape this country's inclination toward tolerance. The fact that the city of Salem has turned the trials into a civic endeavor to preserve the past, as well as an economic stimulant for the community, has not hurt. Increased interest in the occult has increased interest in the trials, and antique collecting has also introduced many to Salem's past.

The Salem Witch trials are one of those unsolved mysteries, or crimes that linger on in peoples minds. Who was Jack the Ripper? Did Lizzie Borden really kill her parents? Where did turn-of-the-century safe cracker Langdon Moore bury the money? Were there really witches in Salem? These are some of the mysteries that intrigue scholars, amateur detectives, historians, and who-done-it lovers.

Does it matter if there were witches in Salem? Even if there were, could or would they have done the things they were accused of? Did the punishment fit the crime? How does one justify the ruination of lives, and the taking of so many lives, including that of a dog which was hung. The victims were not allowed to defend themselves against real, solid facts, only hysterical allegations.

Today we can be grateful that our laws don't allow such things as spectral witnesses (a ghost or dead person that appears to someone like your next door neighbor, who covets your property, and says that you killed someone with a witch's spell.). How would you defend yourself against such an allegation? You know you are innocent but the deck is stacked against you and you are not allowed a lawyer, and you might not be able to afford one even if you were allowed one. What would you do? What could you do? What could those accused over three hundred years ago do? Ignorance, superstition, pride, and avarice predominated in that society. And if you were a woman, elderly, poor, cranky, or eccentric, you were already half guilty of anything that you could be accused of. If you were fortunate enough to have family and friends who were loving and caring, then you fared much better. If life was harsh and bitter for men, it was doubly so for women.

Those whose innocent blood was spilt shall not be forgotten but remembered, cherished, and honored. Their demise opened the paths of progress, tolerance, understanding, suffrage, and civil rights. In 1957, the Commonwealth of Massachusetts reversed the stigma placed on all those who had not been cleared by previous orders.

In 1958, a woman was put to death in Mexico for committing witchcraft.

Hung on Gallows Hill:

Bridget Bishop of Salem June 10
Sarah Good from Salem Village, July 19
Elizabeth Howe from Ipswich, July 19
Rebecca Nourse from Salem Village, July 19
Susannah Martin From Amesbury, July 19
Sarah Wides from Topsfield, July 19
Rev. George Burroughs from Wells, August 19
Margaret Currier from Andover, August 19
George Jacobs from Salem, August19
John Proctor from Salem Village August 19
John Willard from Salem Village, August 19
Martha Corey from Salem Village September 22
Mary Estey from Topsfield, September 22
Alice Parker from Salem, September 22
Mary Parker from Andover, Sept ember 22
Ann Pudeater from Salem, September22
Wilmot Reed from Marblehead, September 22
Margaret Scott from Rowley, September 22
Samuel Wardwell from Andover, September 22

In addition, Giles Corey of Salem Farms was pressed to death. Ann Foster and Sarah Osburn died in jail. It is known that others, including children, also met their demise in jail due to harsh treatment. In all, twenty people were executed and one-hundred-and-fifty were accused and jailed, including nine children aged five to fourteen. Two hundred more had accusations outstanding and fifty confessed, though many recanted later.

Massassachuetts was torn by fear, ignorance, and intrigue. The winter of 1691–92 was not a particularly good time for the settlers of this English colony. Indians frequently attacked, the weather and crops had not been the best, and chances were you would wake up one morning and find you had been "called out" by the "poor afflicted children" who pointed you out as a witch.

The intolerance and inflexibility of the stern, fundamentalist Puritans were being bolstered by the wilderness and deprivations of colony life, where threats and hardships had to be faced daily. Fear was as much a reality as the dangers that lurked for the colonists, and life was gray and grim. Puritans worked six days a week, from dawn to dusk. They never sang or danced, and had sex only for purposes of procreation. On Sundays they switched gears a little, spending the entire day listening to hellfire, brimstone, and damnation warnings about what happened to those who strayed even a smidgen from the rules of the Puritan church. The poet Dante would have felt at home in Salem. The work the men did was probably agrarian, and back breaking, and behind every tree lurked a bear, wildcat, or Indian. For women it was even more difficult bearing children year after year, and many did not survive. Those who survived childbirth raised the

Pertinent pages from the 1893 catalogue. *From the collection of Connie Halket.* $95 for complete catalogue.

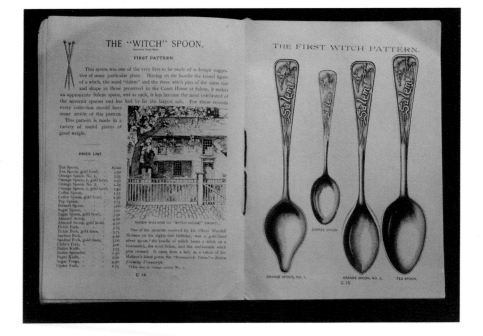

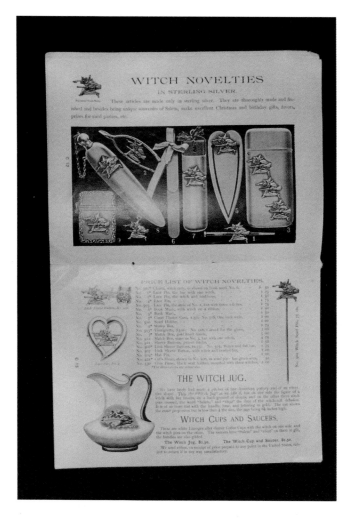

WITCH NOVELTIES

IN STERLING SILVER.

These articles are made only in sterling silver. They are thoroughly made and finished and besides being unique souvenirs of Salem, make excellent Christmas and birthday gifts, favors, prizes for card parties, etc.

PRICE LIST OF WITCH NOVELTIES.

No. 301* Charm, witch only, as shown on book mark No. 8, $ .50
No. 1* Lace Pin, the bar with one witch, 1.25
No. 2* Lace Pin, the witch and hairbrow, 1.25
No. 3* Lace Pin, 1.25
No. 303. Lace Pin, in the style of No. 2, but with three witches, 2.75
No. 8* Book Mark, with witch on a ribbon, 3.50
No. 4* Book Mark, 2.50
No. 5* Card Theatre Case, Little No. 308, One lock with, 4.00
No. 330. Scarf Holder, 1.00
No. 7* Stamp Box, 2.25
No. 313* Vinaigrette, $3.00; No. 316, raised for the glass, 2.50
No. 1* Match Box, gold lined inside, 2.00
No. 312. Match Box, same as No. 3, but with one witch, 1.25
No. 311. Sleeve Buttons, patent slides, 2.50
No. 302* Link Sleeve Buttons, $2.75. No. 302, Witch and dot bar, 1.75
No. 305. Link Sleeve Button, with witch and raised bar, 3.00
No. 309* Hat Pin, 1.50
No. 424* Cuff Pins, shown in No. 307, as scarf pin - has glass eyes, 1.25
No. 430. Glove Purse, black seal leather, mounted with three witches, 3.00
*The illustrations are full size.

No. 309 Witch Scarf Pin, 15 cts.

THE WITCH JUG.

We have lately had made a picture of fine American pottery and of no other fine shape. This the WITCH JUG as we call it, has on one side the figure of a witch with her broom on a back-ground of clouds, and on the other three witch pins crossed, the word "Salem," and "1692" the date of the witchcraft delusion. It is of an ivory tint with the handle, base, and lettering in gold. The cut shows the exact proportions but is less than the size, the jug being 6½ inches high.

WITCH CUPS AND SAUCERS.

These are white Limoges after dinner Coffee Cups with the witch on one side and the witch pins on the other. The names have "Salem" and "1692" on them in gold, the handles are also gilded.

The Witch Jug, $1.50.   **The Witch Cup and Saucer, $1.50.**

We send either, on receipt of price prepaid to any point in the United States, subject to return if in any way unsatisfactory.

15

children and nursed them through illnesses, wove cloth on a loom and sewed clothing, churned the butter, salted and cured meat, cooked the meals, collected and dried herbs, and preserved food for winter use. The chores were enormous in scope.

Today washing clothing is a relatively easy task—we throw the clothing and the soap into a machine and, presto, clean clothes. In 1691 you scrubbed on a rock with cold water and homemade lye soap,.then rinsed it and hung it to dry. You cooked with a fireplace, which warmed the house in the winter and made it a sheer hell in the summertime. Homegrown chickens had to be killed, plucked, and cleaned before they could be spitted over the fire and eaten. Corn had to be hand shucked from the ear and then ground. In short, nothing was easy. It was all hard work which started before dawn and ended after dark. There were no dances, or movies, or friendly little get-togethers for cards, or an evening of friendly exchanges over a nice mellow wine.

It was not only a social disgrace for a woman of childbearing age to remain single, it was just not allowed. If you were a widow you remarried as quickly as possible. Men required a strong-backed woman to work for them and women needed protection from Indians, pirates, and wild animals. Affection and sex were frowned upon by society.

Even those who were comfortably settled in or lived in the cities and were not rural or farm people had difficult lives. The sea played a major part in the economic survival of New England. The wife of a fisherman, whaler, or seaman had more than her share of burdens to bare. Salem was a seafaring town and a major port from whence ships sailed and often never returned.

Is it any wonder that the witch trials came to fruit in this repressed and harsh society? Is it possible that, in this atmosphere of hardship, fear, and repression, the hysteria of the trials was inevitable? Lack of education, creature comforts, and the uncertainty of life were difficult enough. Coupled with superstition and chicanery, things could only go from bad to worse.

Salem Village was the area known as Danvers today. Salem is the city itself.

The Reverend Samuel Parris, arrived in Salem at a time when there was much dissension in the area. The Reverend Burroughs had left because of the factional fighting in the town and had taken a position in Maine. Parris was an opportunist and totally different from his predecessor. He arrived in Salem just after a drought and corn blight had wiped out much of the crop.

There was political turmoil—the liberal governor of Massachusetts had left and everyone was awaiting a new governor and who knew what type of new repressions. The loss of a liberal charter could only cause uncertainty, as did the heavy new taxes. If the residents were unhappy because of the smallpox epidemic, or the cold hard winter, they were even more unhappy when the new minister made himself unpopular with a large portion of his congregation. A boundary dispute which had caused a schism between many of the residents continued on and Parris—described as a humorless, harsh, odious, foul tempered, stingy, mean, unbending, demanding, and crafty man—did not make himself a salve or balm on the many wounds, real or imagined, suffered by his flock. This was definitely not the shepherd the congregation needed.

A Harvard dropout, Parris did not have the education that was expected in a Puritan minister. What he did have was the savvy of a merchant who had lived in the West Indies for years, making his living selling various commodities including molasses, rum, slaves, bibles, and sugar. It was all the same to him. When he came to Salem he brought with him two slaves who would play a role in the mischief that was to follow. Parris did not command the great respect a Puritan minister should and his detractors outnumbered his supporters. This made him bitter. His supporters, often as not, were those who felt they might gain by staying in his good graces.

It is interesting to know that Rebecca Nourse was one of the villagers who strongly opposed Parris becoming minister. She further incurred his wrath by opposing the "cryings out" or accusations, and she boycotted a church meeting that Parris called. Nourse might have been a seventy-one-year-old matron, but she was well liked and respected and very literate when most people were not.

Parris was quite close with Thomas Putnam and the two men fed off of each other. Putnam wanted land and wealth and Parris wanted wealth, position, and respect. Thomas Putnam's daughter, Ann, was one of the "afflicted children" and his wife, Ann, an extremely neurotic woman, later joined the group of "afflicted" girls who blamed their ills on witchcraft. Thomas Putnam wanted desperately to consolidate the borders of his property. Was he above sacrificing his family to do so?

Cotton Mather desperately wanted to follow in the footsteps of his father and outsine him by becoming the next chancellor of Harvard. He was a self-styled authority on witchcraft and wrote many books on the subject. He fanned the flames of discontent and his hubris knew no bounds. Sitting on his horse watching the execution of the Reverend George Burroughs and others, he incited the crowds and harangued the soon-to-be-hung with cries of "repent and confess." His charity and sympathetic nature were hardly tempered by Christian love. Even after the whole tragedy was over, Mather still insisted the devil was in New England and it was all the devil's fault. No wonder many thought the devil was Cotton Mather and his cronies. His reputation wasn't helped after Robert Calef wrote *More Wonders of the Invisible World*, a pamphlet that opened the eyes of many New Englanders to the fanaticism of men like Cotton Mather and the injustice they could incite. The pamphlet, in addition to Mather's refusal to take any blame for what had happened, not only made him a laughing stock, but caused him to lose the coveted Harvard position.

Magistrates John Hathorne and Jonathan Corwin and court clerk Ezekiel Cheever were prejudiced beyond all bounds. Leading questions, lack of legal representation, and use of spectral evidence made it possible to intimidate the accused and to confuse them. Some poor wretches confessed because they felt so intimidated. It was difficult enough for an educated woman who was sharp as a needle, like Rebecca Nourse, who had benefit of all her senses and a loving

Daniel Low catalogue for 1908, showing pertinent pages for Salem witch items for sale. *From the collection of Susan Erickson.* $85 for complete catalogue.

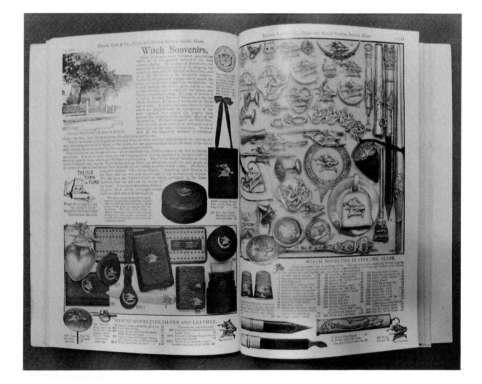

18

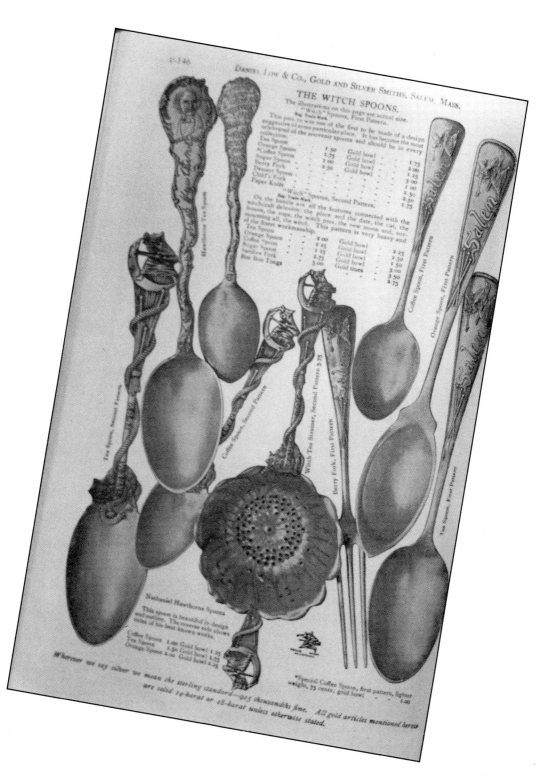

supportive family. However, it was easy to use leading questions to trap women who were not well educated, or were senile, or slaves, or small children. Plus, Cheever added all types of incriminating remarks to the court records.

Of the seven jurists named to the bench, not one of them was formally trained in the law and most prepared themselves for the job by reading a few books on witchcraft. Samuel Sewall became the most "famous" of the seven on the special court of Oyer and Terminer. Nathaniel Saltonstall, Bartholomew Gedney, and deputy governor William Stoughton made up the balance. Cotton Mather produced a paper called "Return of Several Ministers" which influenced these men and set them on the course which would cost their fellow human beings life, liberty, and material possessions.

Abigail Williams, the niece of Samuel Parris, and his daughter, Betty, were two of the "afflicted" children. The others were Mary Warren, Mercy Lewis, Sarah Churchill, Mary Walcott, Elizabeth Booth, Ann Putnam (later joined by her mother, Mrs. Ann Putnam), Elizabeth Hubbard, and Suzannaah Sheldon. They were all part of a group called "the Circle" which met at the Reverend Parris's home. They were all supposed to be pious young women doing only what the Puritan society would allow them to do and approve of and yet, ... one night, a few of them were caught dancing in the moonlight. Then, the following day, Betty Parris fell ill with fever and hallucinations.

These hallucinations may well have gotten their start in Parris's home. Parris brought two slaves with him from the islands—John Indian and his wife, Tituba. She was apparently well versed in voodoo and the stories she told the girls and the fortune readings she did, incited them to press her for more forbidden information. She often did spells. Later both she and her husband were accused of witchcraft and she freely confessed and involved other people in the web that would become more intricate as time went by. Tituba, in the end, was one of the few "winners" in the whole affair. Hating the cold climate of New England and the stern, fanatical Puritans, she was quietly sold off by Parris to pay her prison fees and sent back to the warm Caribbean.

Prison fees and all charges had to be born by the accused. Chains, food, the use of the bug-ridden jail cell, etc., were not courtesy of the colony. The accused was made to pay for everything, including being tortured. Those who could not were denied access to even the merest food and blankets. Is it any wonder that people died in jail? Even after the general amnesty some were kept in jail because they could not pay. One woman became an indentured servant in order to leave jail. Imagine signing away your freedom in order to get out of jail for a crime you were acquitted of and should never have been charged with.

The Reverend George Burroughs was a small man, but very strong. So strong that it was considered unnatural and therefore he had to be a witch. Once the minister of Salem, he had left the village an unpopular man with the Putnams and others. He had considerable prejudice against him when the girls cried out his name. Pulled from his home in Wells, Maine, in the middle of winter, and dragged back to Salem, his seven children, the eldest being sixteen, were turned out to fend for themselves in the dead of winter by the current Mrs. Burroughs, their stepmother and a devout Puritan. The children's survival was due to charity, luck, perseverance, and divine provenance.

Burroughs protested his innocence, but the court convicted him despite the fact he could recite the Lord's Prayer. (It was a well known fact that witches could not say the "Lord's Prayer," except maybe backwards.) As he stood on the gallows ready to be hung, he recited the "Lord's Prayer again and aroused the crowd to protest his hanging. The officials had their way. The short minister with extraordinary strength and great pride in it, was hung with the rest, leaving his children penniless orphans in the wilderness.

Bridget Bishop was a prime target to be called out. She wore red on her bodice and petticoats, owned and ran two successful taverns, fought with both of her husbands, was rumored to be of poor moral character, and did not comply with the strict tenants of behavior the church had set for how a woman should act. She played shovelboard, got into fist fights, spoke her mind, flirted, and in general was a liberated free spirit. And that was not acceptable. No wonder she was cried out against by more people than any other. Much of this was envy and the attacks against her in court were directed as much toward her lifestyle and lack of piety than anything else.

Elizabeth Proctor's life was spared because she was pregnant. By the time she delivered her child in prison the executions had been halted. Her husband, John, did not fare so well. He refused to take the "afflicted" girls seriously and to protect his wife, said he'd had carnal knowledge of Parris's neice, Abigail Williams. This offense, having carnal knowledge of someone you were not married to, was a serious crime in the Puritan colonies, but the court didn't believe him and said he was lying because the devil was his master. Interestingly enough, the last reports of Abigail Williams are that she was earning her living on the docks in a socially unexceptable way.

It is not only possible but probably that John Proctor knew her sexually and was willing to sacrifice his life and his reputation by confessing that sexual laison in order to, hopefully, stop the mayhem he felt was going on. He knew then that there wasn't a chance of getting a fair trial, especially after he wrote to ministers in Boston, imploring them to intercede in the case of his wife, and they refused to help. Of course, they wouldn't—Cotton Mather influenced what those ministers said and did.

There were others who, like John Proctor, took a stand against the court and its proceedings. Some chose to flee New England rather than experience the same fate. Philip and Mary English, Edward and Sarah Bishop, Elizabeth and Nathaniel Cary, and John and Dudley Badstreet all escaped. Mary Bradbury, unlike the others, had already been condemned when she escaped. Even though he was well known and powerful, John Alden chose to escape rather than face trial. He knew he could not win against a stacked jury.

The only judge who resigned because he was so disgusted with what was happening and thought the children were "blind, nonsensical, girls" was Nathaniel Saltonstall. Unfortunately, he didn't have the courage of his convictions to stand up to the other judges in a public protest as he might have been able to mobilize public opinion. Perhaps he didn't because another man who tried to discredit the afflicted girls, Robert Pike, had failed and been forced to run away. Saltonstall knew the power of those girls and it may have been fear that made him abstain from such an action. Fear is terrible thing.

Giles Corey was not the most amiable and kindly person and must have been a very difficult person to live with. It is partly his fault that his wife, Martha, was called out as a witch and his testimony was certainly unfavorable, if not damning to her. Therefore it's not surprising that this stubborn old man chose not to plead when he himself was called out upon. What must he have thought when they started to place rocks on his chest to force a confession? How did he feel being so tortured for the same crime he had confirmed his wife was guilty of?

Laws were different in the 1690s. If you refused to plead guilty or not guilty you were tortured or pressed until you made a plea. Corey might have refused to plead so they could not touch his property and assets. It is hard to believe anyone could submit to such a painful ordeal just to protect their property. When he told them with his dying words, "Pile more (rocks) on" did he realize the enormity of his actions in helping convict his wife of Witchcraft? Had he any remorse for the way his wife, Martha, died? Hanging might be quicker, but she had a trial, the betrayal of a husband, and the depravation of prison to suffer through, while his were only a few days of exquisite pain before he died. Perhaps he alone of all the accused had something to repent of.

There are so many characters and people whose stories belong in this chapter. It is impossible to tell their stories as this is a book on collectibles and not on the trials.

In order to appreciate the collectibles you must try and understand the fascination of this small vignette of history and how it influenced not only the participants but future generations. This short, atrocious chapter of history has maintained its allure and, as thousands flock to the historic landmarks every year, the souvenirs from the early years will continue to draw great interest. Because so many of these trinkets and tiny objects fall into the collecting categories of so many different collections and interests, the value will always be there and the desire for the items will continue to grow as new generations of tourists discover the mystery of one of the great "who done its" or "why did they do its" of all time.

This is the teaspoon that started the souvenir spoon collecting craze; the spoon without which no collection is complete. $95.

Here is an actual sign from the historic trail. This sign was obviously used at one time to denote the tenth stop on the historic trail. It is made of sheet steel with a silk-screened design in green. The red "10" was painted on and it is assumed that others exist with other numbers on them. They were believed to still be in use in the early 1950s. Unfortunately, this one suffered a few gunshot wounds. $150.

Reflections on Old Salem Town

A POEM

An infant was born in a prison cell
its mother accused, a witch
its father hung before he was born
because he held Parris and Mather in scorn.
Seven children were turned out of their warm Maine home,
when father was dragged back to old Salem town,
Alas, he knew hubris in being exceptionally strong.
Stepmother didn't care it was winter and cold,
she didn't want witch's brats or mangy old cats,
mercy and charity—she just didn't care for that.
Small children confessed they knew witches,
and they themselves were
small children who didn't realize just what witches were.
Old women, some loved, some not, where hung on a hill by the executioner's
knot.
Be quiet and hide lest you, too, be cried out on
as you go about your chores one cold early morn,
thinking to hide from malice, ignorance, and ministerial pride.
Old and young chained in a cold jail cell
no place to sleep and not much to eat.
Some lived there, some died there, others went to hang on Gallows Hill.
So many lives ruined there, in old Salem town, and their ghosts haunt there still.
Their faith was strong and their God wasn't wrong,
it was just religion gone sour, and ministerial power.
The witches we hold in high regard,
the ministers and magistrates deserve to rest uneasy in the cold ground.

PART 2

Collectibles

Silverware

Orange spoon. Bowl shapes changed but were often used for the same function. $125.

Small spoon, possibly for feeding a youth. $125.

Sugar spoon with ornate bowl. $145.

Spoon, usage uncertain, perhaps a pap spoon. $85.

Enameled demitasse spoon, white and pale blue with a streak of pale yellow enamel on the handle. $95.

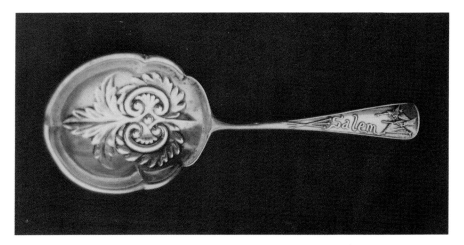

Bonbon spoon with ornate bowl. $145.

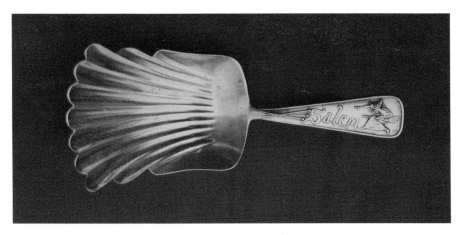

A wonderful nut scoop. $150.

Salt spoon made by Payne and Baker. $75.

Bonbon shovel. $75.

The bowl on this bonbon spoon is quite ornate. $145.

Strawberry fork. $95.

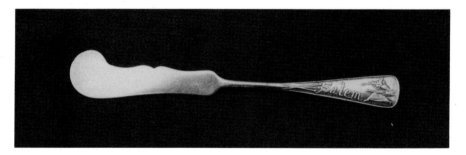

Individual butter knife. $85.

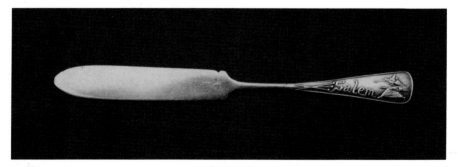

Individual butter spreader. $75.

This double handled tea strainer with poppy flower bowl is one of the most coveted of all tea strainers. $400.

One couldn't ask for a nicer piece than this double-handled tea strainer, made to be used with loose tea leaves, placed on the cup so the hot tea could be poured through it. $375.

Sugar tongs. *From the Susan Erickson collection.* $125.

Orange or citrus spoon. $85.

A lovely sterling dish with a heavily embossed witch in the center. Surprisingly enough there is not a maker's mark. $175.

Teaspoon made by the Gorham Silver Company. $125.

This orange spoon had a gilt bowl to keep the citric acid from pitting the spoon. $125

Demitasse spoon with gilt bowl. $75.

Sardine fork $150.

Fancy sugar shell. $145.

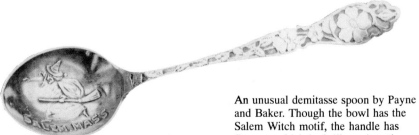

An unusual demitasse spoon by Payne and Baker. Though the bowl has the Salem Witch motif, the handle has flowers, which look like poinsettias and give it a Christmas feel. $50.

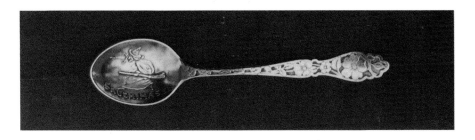

Another flower-handled spoon by Payne and Baker. These spoons were from their regular line and the witch was stamped into the bowl with a die. $45.

A 1970s-type, base metal spoon with a witch above a banner proclaiming "Salem." $10.

This is another Payne and Baker stock spoon with an Indian handle. It is smaller and lighter than most demitasse spoons. Even the witch motif is unusual—though it is stamped in the bowl along with "Salem, Mass.," the figure is more like the old lady who swept the cobwebs from the sky than the usual Salem witch on a broom. $40

33

Kings Pattern Whiting 1893 spoon with bright cut bowl of witch. *From the collection of Connie Halket.* $55.

Bright cut bowl of the Witch House with goldenrod handle. No maker's mark. *From the collection of Connie Halket.* $45.

Enameled commemorative spoon made for the Northeastern Spoon Collectors Guild in 1997. *From the collection of Connie Halket.* $10.

Souvenir spoon made in 1970 with a cutout witch design at the top. Made by J. T. Inman. *From the collection of Connie Halket.* $35.

Front and reverse of the souvenir spoon for the hundredth anniversary of the original Number 1 souvenir witch spoon. This, of course, is the Number 2 design. It is not cut out and commemorative information is on the reverse side. Made for the Northeastern Spoon Collectors Guild. *From the collection of Connie Halket.* $45.

Enamel pin from spoon convention in 1990. *From the collection of Connie Halket.* $10.

Pin back button of the souvenir centenary in 1990. *From the collection of Connie Halket.* $5.

𝕵𝖊𝖜𝖊𝖑𝖗𝖞

Sterling witch on wishbone pin. $65.

Sterling witch on moon pin. $50.

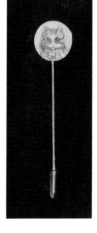

This cat stickpin is shown in Low catalogues without the green rhinestone eyes. They are, however, original to the item, as the piece was produced with and without the glass eyes. *From the collection of Susan Erickson.* $45.

A tiny witch charm. $35.

Small witch charm. *From the collection of Connie Halket.* $35.

A pair of cufflinks with a cat face on one side and a witch on the other. *From the collection of Susan Erickson.* $75.

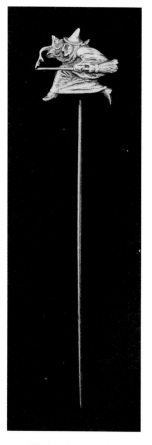

Witch stick pin. $45.

Sterling witch on knot. $65.

The same witch without the knot, half of a cufflink or could be used as a charm. $15.

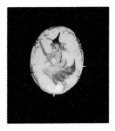

A sweet little china lapel pin with the Upton design witch on it. $45.

Winslow Lewis K. T. (Knights Templer, affiliated with the Masonic order) 26th Triennial Conclave, 1895 pin. Made of base metal and plated. Nice die-cut design of the witch. Manufactured by F. L. Logee & Co. Providence, R.I. $35.

Tie clip from 1925, obviously made for some special occasion. $45.

Cups, Saucers, and Assorted Chinaware

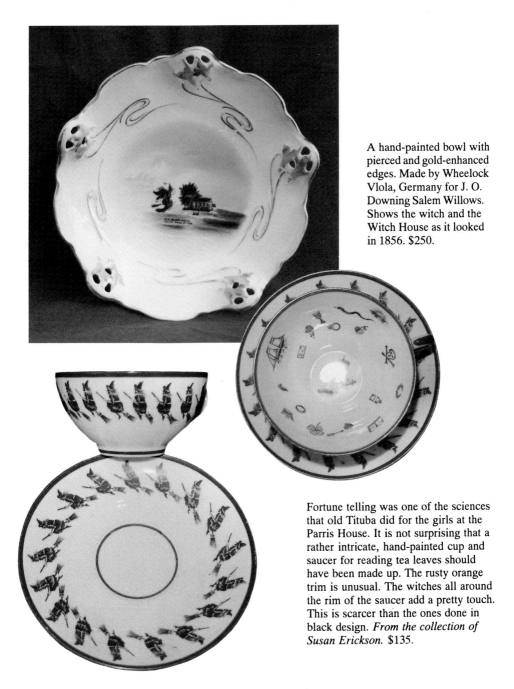

A hand-painted bowl with pierced and gold-enhanced edges. Made by Wheelock Vlola, Germany for J. O. Downing Salem Willows. Shows the witch and the Witch House as it looked in 1856. $250.

Fortune telling was one of the sciences that old Tituba did for the girls at the Parris House. It is not surprising that a rather intricate, hand-painted cup and saucer for reading tea leaves should have been made up. The rusty orange trim is unusual. The witches all around the rim of the saucer add a pretty touch. This is scarcer than the ones done in black design. *From the collection of Susan Erickson.* $135.

A heavy gold rim adorns this transfer design of the Salem witch. Made for Daniel Low.

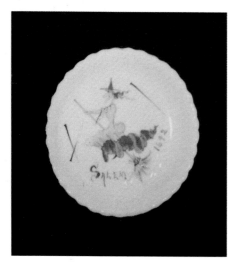

A small round dish hand painted by Upton. *From the collection of Susan Erickson.* $55.

Two variations of the same Salem souvenir plate. Though the flowing blue is much more attractive than the red, it is not as scarce, but more desirable On the lower right is the Witch House and at the top, the witch logo.The blue plate is marked England. The red one is marked "Old English Staffordshire Ware." Made by Adams for Salem Harbor Gift Shop, Salem. $135 each.

Three variations of the same plate. The green is the scarcest and unmarked, but the flowing blue is the most desirable. The gold trim on the plates must have been applied very thinly as it is almost always very worn. The 6-inch plate was made by Rowland & Marsellus Co. Staffordshire, England. The 8-inch plate was designed and imported by Daniel Low and made by Frank Beardsmore & Co., Fenton, England. $125-150 each.

This is very similar to the preceding three plates, yet with a very different border. It is also less flat and more plate-like. $145.

A nice large witch in the center with Salem scenes around the border. The Witch House at the bottom is where the trials took place. Marked "England." $125.

A nicely designed witch in the center, but the border seems out of character. Obviously the rim was a stock pattern. Designed by Daniel Low and made by Beardsmore & Co. Fenton, England. $125.

A pale blue souvenir plate with the witch greatly reduced in the center. The Witch House is on the right.

A large creamer painted by Upton from a T&V (Limoges) Touraine, France blank. *From the collection of Debbie Dwyer.* $95.

The Hampshire Pottery witch pitcher is one of the most desirable pieces made by that company. They produced the same shape with other pictures on it, though the witch motif is the most desirable. Blanks were made, so it is very important to check and see if the picture is under the glaze. A picture over the glaze is not original to the piece. The gold trim on these did not wear well. The back view shows the infamous pins which still exist today and were supposedly those stuck into the bewitched girls by the witches. $500.

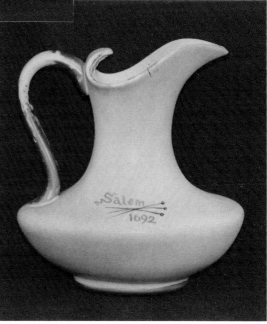

The Hampshire Pottery milk pitcher has a handle on the back and the spout on the side. This piece very rarely shows up with the witch motif. Impressed with Hampshire mark. $800.

Plate with transfer design of the Witch House in the center and gold trim. Made in Germany for A.B. Russell, Salem. $50.

A demitasse showing the Upton witch.

The cup on this transfer-design demitasse has the Witch House on it and the saucer has the House of Seven Gables, which was erected in 1670. It is quite common for different places in the same town to be shown together as it would make it saleable in more than one tourist spot. As both places were tourist meccas, they compliment each other nicely. Made in Germany for A. B. Russell. $50.

The motif on these two transfer-design demitasse are the same, but the shapes are very different. Carlsbad China, Austria, for Frank Cousins. $75 each.

This is a much fancier coffee cup and
saucer with a pressed-daisy petal design
in the saucer and on the fluted cup. The
Witch House is on the cup. Made in
Germany for A. B. Russell. $75.

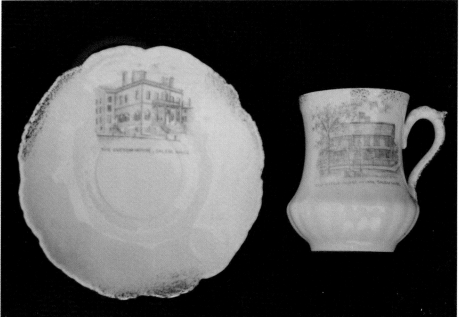

A nice green transfer design on demitasse. The cup shows the Witch House. Carlsbad China,
Austria. The Custom House is pictured on the saucer. $40.

Two different sizes of a fortune-telling cup and saucer with a sailing ship (Salem was a port catering to whalers and other sailing ships), a snake, ring, four-leaf clover, joined hearts, skull and cross bones, etc. $75 each.

Demitasse for historic Salem. Transfer design probably from the 1960s. $15.

An individual creamer with a transfer of the old Witch House. $50.

Individual creamers like this were inexpensive because they were transfer designs rather than hand painted and were quite popular with the tourists.B F H S China, Austria, for Almy Bigelow & Washburn, Salem. $60.

A rather clumsy milk pitcher with a transfer design of the Witch House on one side and the House of Seven Gables on the other. Made in Austria for Frank Cousins. $65.

A small pin dish with a transfer design. Made in Austria for Frank Cousins. $25.

A pin dish with transfer design. Made in Austria for Frank Cousins by Carlsbad China. *From the Michael Michaud collection.* $25.

The same transfer design decorated very differently. Orange rim for J.C. Downing, other for Frank Cousins. $25 each.

Back of a Wedgwood plate showing the witch logo and "Made in England for Daniel Low & Co. Salem makers of the Witch spoons." The logo for Jones McDuffee & Stratton, sole importers, is also on the plate. $85.

A free-form, small dish with the witch transfer in the center. Marked "Daniel Low." $40.

A footed candlestick with handle and hand-painted witch. Signed Upton. $125.

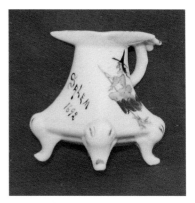

Cup plate with the Upton design witch on it. *From the collection of Connie Halket.* $65.

A transfer toothpick holder with gold trim. Carlsbad China, made in Austria for Frank Cousins. $55.

Blue Salem Souvenir plate with leaf border, shows the Witch House on the right. England. $75.

Besides being a wonderful example of enameled glass, this is one of the most colorful items made for the witch trade. Gold is used to enhance the design and for the rim. $150.

A tall candlestick, hand painted by Upton. *From the collection of Susan Erickson.* $145.

Bottled Goods

Bottles maintaining their original label are hard to find. Superior Lubricating Oil, made by the Salem Chemical Company, could be used for everything from sewing machines to guns. *From the collection of Michael Michaud.* $50.

A nicely embossed Witch Cream bottle from Price Druggist, with original metal screw-on cap. Earlier bottles were simply corked. $35.

Witch Hazel, a four-ounce bottle at fourteen percent alcohol, made by Salem Chemical & Supply Co. Paper labels on bottles are prized by collectors. $45.

Luscomb's Witch Liquid Smelling Salts were sold in this fabulous teal bottle with an embossed witch on the front and the stopper. Embossing was used not only for design but so that you would know from touch that the item contained poison. The raised stopper indicated that the contents were not for consumption. $350.

W.C.B. Wks, Inc., one-pint, 10-ounce jar. This is a nicer witch figure than most, larger, and nicely executed. $55.

Front and back of a ten-inch-tall, clear bottle by J. E. H. Witch City Bottling Works sports a very skinny witch. Embossed and registered. $45.

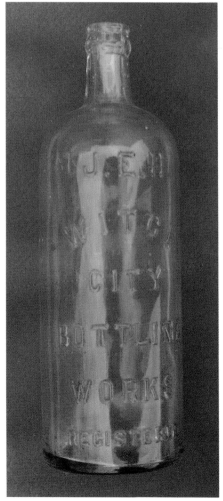

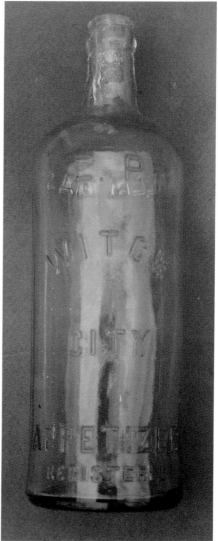

Front and reverse of E.P. Witch City
Appetizer. $45.

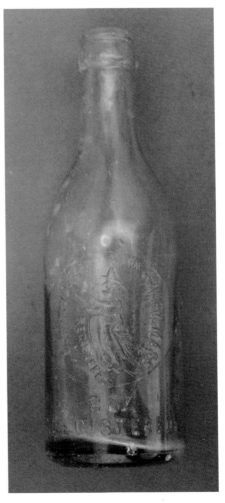

J. Edward Hennessy with slight amethyst tinge to bottle. $15.

E. Provo, eight-ounce bottle. Reverse says "This bottle not to be sold." Nicely embossed, with many stretch marks in the glass. $20.

Miscellaneous

Witchwood Milk bar individual creamer. $40.

A charming, German-made cobalt vase with a hand-painted witch flying over Salem. *From the Susan Erickson collection.* $65.

A celluloid box showing the Witch House. It is not unusual that so many items show the Upton Drug Store as it was part of the attraction and sold souvenirs as well as drugs. The drugstore was an addition to the Witch House that has since been removed. *From the collection of Susan Erickson.* $95.

Sarah W. Symonds made many plaster items for sale. This witch stirring a cauldron was well versed in her Shakespeare. $85.

The witch on this larger, 8-by-5-inch plaque by Sarah Symonds is the same as the smaller, round one. $85.

What material this is made of is a bit of a mystery, but it feels like a limestone with a gritty finish. It is unmarked and does not have any means to hang the piece, besides being too heavy. It is embossed so it can not be used as a trivet. Regardless, it is an interesting item and was sold in the shops in Salem. $65.

This round, 2 1/2-inch Sarah Symonds chalk-ware plaque is a bit cruder than most of her production items. $55.

The front and back of a clay pipe. The bit would probably have been made of wood. This one was never used and never obtained that smokey patina that only comes with being used. $185.

This ceramic figure was made in 1978 by Sagittarius Studios in Stoneham, Mass. $35.

Made of heavy brass, this is more of a chestnut warmer than a bed warmer. The definition of the witch is crude, yet on the whole it is a beautifully made item. Marked "Made in England" with registry number. $325.

A rare Villeroy and Boch Mettlach coaster for putting one's stein or glass down on. Made for Ye Remembrance Shop by C. M. Duren & Co., Salem. $350.

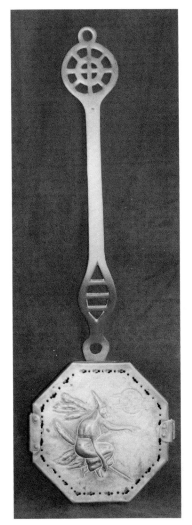

A nicely painted coaster with a pleasant green background and brown rim. Made in Germany. $185.

Usually witches are not depicted as nice looking, but this bisque witch made in Germany is. Painted in very subtle and muted colors, it is one of the most artistic of the Salem pieces. $175.

A heart-shaped box with the Upton Witch painted on it. Very stylized in red and green. One wonders if the artists of this type of piece knew that women didn't wear colors in those days and it was one of the things that Bridget Bishop was condemned for. $145.

Salt and pepper shakers of pot metal with a witch crest sweated on to it. Marked with a large "K" in an oval with "&" to the left of it and "Co." on the other side. $55.

A lovely, hand-painted box large enough to hold a deck of cards. The hole in the bottom is so you could put your finger in and push the deck up and out. The rim has a pink luster. Marked "M.B.N.08" (1908). $165.

Round cardboard box covered with leather, with a silver witch logo in the center. Probably for cufflinks. Marked in the inside but can't be read. $45.

Small dish made of base metal with a wash of copper. Unmarked, but the design is similar to the blue China dishes. $45.

Commemorating the GAR (Grand Army of the Republic) encampment in August 1897 when Post #34 from the Witch City went to Buffalo, New York. Silk ribbon with metal skull holder. $75.

Handmade doll by Mrs Miles. A delightful cloth poppet, not for putting pins in but a keepsake of a time in history when children were not allowed to play with dolls because they were the tools which witches used to torture those they held enmity against. $125.

Double-sided scissors shaped like a witch and made of steel in Germany. $125.

Aluminum pocket knife with design on both sides of the case. Blade marked "Magnetic Cutlery C., Phila., Pa.," on one side (importer?) and "D. Peres, Germany" on reverse (maker?). $35.

A pair of witches, cut from steel, which were meant to be screwed down, perhaps on a hearth. Unmarked but purchased at a church sale years ago in Salem. $150.

The Salem witch thimbles are the most coveted of all thimble designs. Here are three variations enlarged. The logo was stamped with a die on different blanks, so there are variations. $300 each.

Set of five different colored-plastic thimbles. *From the collection of Connie Halket.* $5 set.

Sterling pencil holder with loop so it could be hung from a chain or a chatelaine. The pencil was a small, flat wooden lead pencil which would be inserted into the holder. $75.

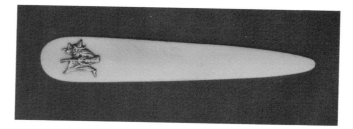

Sterling witch on a celluloid letter opener. $45.

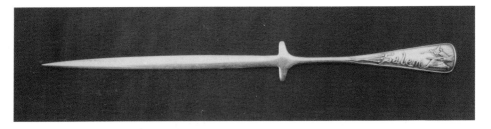

Sterling letter opener with very sharp point. $150.

An advertising trade card given out with the compliments of the Salem Witches, obviously for the election of 1888. The card declares that "We vote the Straight Republican Ticket" and then quotes Gilbert and Sullivan: "And so do our sisters and our cousins and our aunts." Considering the fact that women couldn't vote and had almost as few rights as they did during the witchcraft trials, it is quite a surprising declaration. Could there be some underlying meaning to the fact that the woman pictured wears a jester's outfit? One wonders what the early suffragists thought of the card. The meaning and reason behind this card will probably remain an enigma. $45.

Sterling letter opener. $200.

A marvelous, hinged stamp box with a witch on the front. $150.

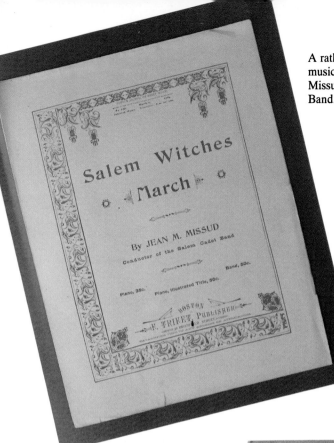

A rather plain version of the sheet music, "Salem Witches March" by Jean Missud, conductor of the Salem Cadet Band.

The Witch House, a 1948 booklet by Fred A. Gannon. $8.

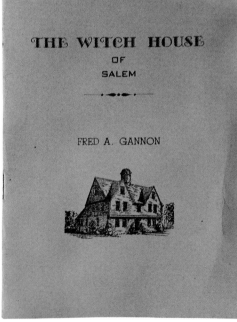

The front and back cover of a piece of sheet music, "March of the Salem Witches," by Jean Michaud, dedicated to the Winslow Lewis Commandery K. T. (Knights Templer). The reverse is an advertisement for Daniel Low and shows two stickpins, a pin, a thimble, #1-pattern strawberry fork, and two styles of teaspoons. This version of the sheet music is scarce; $95.

Giveaway flyers were as common at the turn of the century as they are today. This tri-foldout advertises Witch Cream, sold by C. H. & J. Price. It urges people to purchase and sell both the Witch Cream and the Witches' Toilet Powder. How could you loose as you could make a hundred percent markup. $20.

Photograph of four views of the Witch house published by Upton and Frisbee. $15.

A beautifully executed, reverse painting on glass of the Witch House above an early mirror. The colors are somber but the frame is nicely colored. Pitting is not unusual on early mirrors like this one. May be a one of a kind. $400.

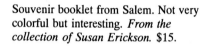

Souvenir booklet from Salem. Not very colorful but interesting. *From the collection of Susan Erickson.* $15.

Witch City Pop Corn. Five ounces of seasoned popcorn, in tin container by R. L'Amontagne, circa 1920s. $100.

Postcards

The postcard is a remarkable method of keeping track of how things change and evolve. Much social and architectural history has been preserved by studying postcards. Alas, there were none done in the days of the trials themselves. Can you imagine the messages that could have been written on them?

The Witch House has been pictured on postcards so often over the years, documenting the many changes of this important site. It is the oldest building in Salem and it was here that the decision was made whether a person would live or die. Sometimes the house was known as the John Alden house, as it was erroneously thought that he lived there for a while. Myths are often difficult to put to sleep. The reason that the trials took place there is that Jonathan Corwin, the main judge, resided there, plus it was centrally located. The "preliminary examinations" began here, and it was all downhill from there, or to risk being crass it was all uphill—to Gallows hill. It is often difficult for people to imagine that this is the same structure that has seen so many changes over the years. The building has been restored and looks the same as when Judge Corwin lived there.

So many publishers and printers have produced cards of this structure that prices are low because they are so common. Prices range between $1 and $6 unless noted.

The Old Parris House is five miles from the Witch House and in 1752 the area was severed from Salem and became Danvers. This is where all the problems started. In 1910, all that remained to remind people of a building that had been "torn down years ago" was a marker. It is not known when this picture of a building, much the worse for wear, was taken, but it looks derelict.

Six views of the home of Rebecca Nourse, built in 1636. The Nourse family actively opposed the trials. When Rebecca, the matriarch of a large family, and her sister, were cried out upon, the family worked to obtain her release and circulated petitions, almost succeeding in saving her from the fate of Gallows Hill. The woman and dog on the one card are superimposed and are not ghosts from 1692. Many of her contemporaries felt Rebecca Nourse to be a true Christian martyr and did not believe her guilty.

REBECCA NURSE HOUSE, BUILT 1636, DANVERS, MASS. REBECCA NURSE WAS HANGED AS A WITCH IN 1692.

1804-M. A. HALL & CO. PUBLISHERS.

Copyright 1905 by the Rotograph Co.
A 6680 Rebecca Nurse House built 1636, (she was hanged as a witch in Salem 1692)
Danvers, Mass.

Rebecca Nurse House, DANVERS, Mass.
(She was hanged for Witchcraft in 1692)

REBECCA NURSE HOUSE, BUILT 1636, DANVERS, MASS.
1804-PUBLISHED BY M. A. HALL & CO.

Danvers, Mass., The Old Nurse House

Danvers, Mass. - Rebecca Nurse House - Hanged for Witchcraft in 1692

Three views of the tombstone of Col. John Hawthorne, the Witch Judge. Notice the death head on the top of the stone. There are some who feel it stands for the people whose lives he helped take. Perhaps, the epitaph should have read differently.

The most fanciful of all the cards. Notice the ribbons on the front of the broom are really snakes. No wonder the man in the moon looks so surprised! $15.

This is how the Sarah Osborn house looked in 1907. The house was built in 1660. The house is in Danvers. Sarah Osborn died in prison, one of the first people called out on by the girls.

Monument to John Proctor, one of the main opponents of the trials. It is probable that he did have a sexual relationship with Abigail Williams and was willing to sacrifice himself to stop what he thought was a travesty. His letter writing and petitioning began in ernest when his wife was accused. Because of his opposition, he too was accused. His wife was spared only because she was pregnant and by the time she delivered her child the executions had stopped. John was not so fortunate. Arthur Miller's play *The Crucible* was based on the story of John Proctor. It has recently been made into a movie.

Views of the oldest and most photographed building in Salem. There is not an angle or a view of it at any period (after the birth of the camera) that was not taken. The building stands at 310 Essex Street and has been restored to the time of the trials. It is interesting to see the additions and changes, the store fronts with signs, the trees as saplings and grown to maturity, and the building without trees. Looking at all these different cards, you might have problems believing it is the same building. The interesting views of the pharmacy—Upton and Frisbee—are fun as one notices Moxie and other advertising signs in the windows.It was here that the initial interrogations took place and it is here that tourists will always come to see where the most famous witch trials since Joan of Arc took place.

OLD WITCH HOUSE, SALEM, MASS

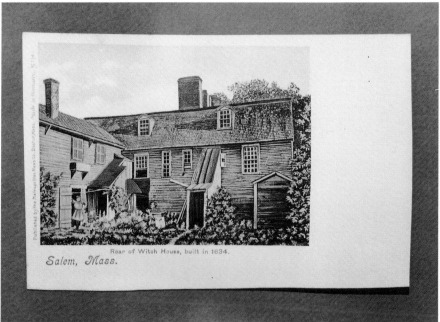

Rear of Witch House, built in 1634.

Salem, Mass.

Witch House, built in 1634, Salem, Mass.

OLD WITCH HOUSE. AFTER 1780. SALEM. MASS.

Old Witch House, Salem, Mass.

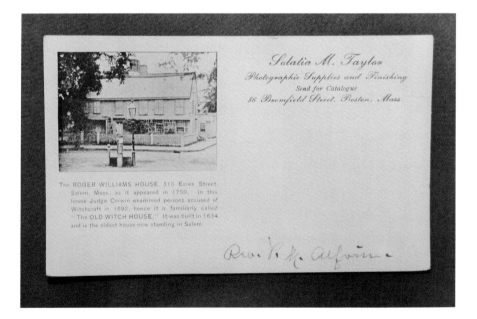

The ROGER WILLIAMS HOUSE, 310 Essex Street, Salem, Mass., as it appeared in 1750. In this house Judge Corwin examined persons accused of Witchcraft in 1692, hence it is familiarly called "The OLD WITCH HOUSE." It was built in 1634 and is the oldest house now standing in Salem.

Solatia M. Taylor
Photographic Supplies and Finishing
Send for Catalogue
56 Bromfield Street, Boston, Mass.

Sat nion
Salam
Dear Emily
I am not
gung to write
any more till
you write a
long letter
I wrote you
two long ones
Love to Pa & Ma
Cella

127 OLD WITCH HOUSE, SALEM, MASS., AS IT WAS UP TO 1856

ROGER WILLIAMS
Old Witch House, Salem, Mass.

WITCH HOUSE, SALEM, MASS.

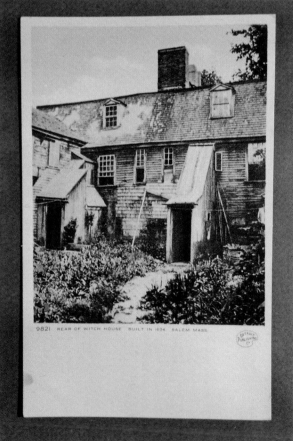

9821 REAR OF WITCH HOUSE BUILT IN 1634 SALEM MASS.

Salem, Mass. Rear of Witch House.

Rear of Witch House, built in 1634.

Salem, Mass.

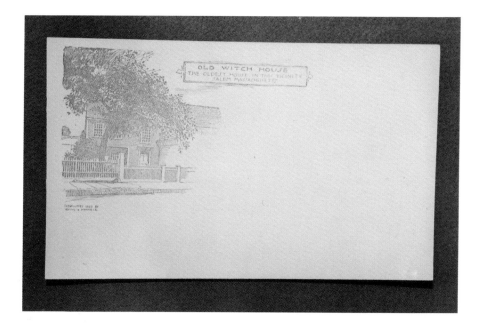

Old Witch House, Salem, Mass.

WITCH HOUSE, SALEM, MASS

9727 OLD WITCH HOUSE SALEM MASS

MAIN ENTRANCE, OLD WITCH HOUSE BUILT 1635, SALEM, MASS.

Witch House,
Salem, Mass.

10191 OLD WITCH HOUSE SALEM MASS.   WHERE VICTIMS OF WITCHCRAFT WERE CONDEMNED 1692.

Copyright 1905 by the Rotograph Co.
A 0586 Roger Williams House or Old Witch House, built 1635, Salem, Mass.

WITCH HOUSE, SALEM, MASS.
#201. COPYRIGHT, 1901, BY DETROIT PHOTOGRAPHIC CO.

9727. OLD WITCH HOUSE, SALEM, MASS.

Salem, Mass. Roger Williams House or Witch House.
Ye Oldest House in Salem. Erected before 1635.

The Old Witch House, built in 1635, Salem, Mass.

97

OLD WITCH HOUSE, AFTER 1780, SALEM, MASS

Old Witch House

Greetings from
Salem, Mass.

July 19

Dear Bowman

We are in a very beautiful old town where they used to hang persons for being witches. So it is sometimes called the "Witch City." I have charge of the Church here through July. I hope the fishes are biting better than they did. Love to all. Admittedly, M. A. Tolman

WITCH HOUSE, SALEM, MASS.

WITCH HOUSE, SALEM, MASS.

The Witch House, built in 1634, Salem, Mass.

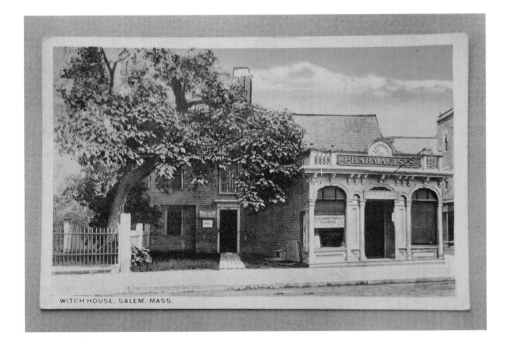

WITCH HOUSE, SALEM, MASS.

ROGER WILLIAMS OR WITCH HOUSE, ERECTED BEFORE 1635, SALEM, MASS.

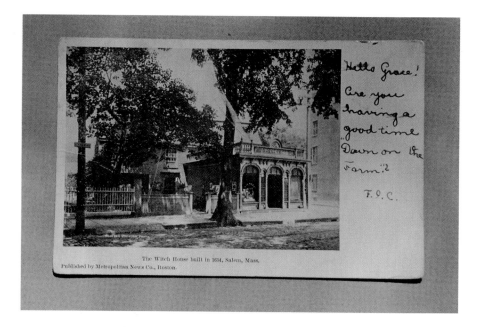

The Witch House built in 1634, Salem, Mass.
Published by Metropolitan News Co., Boston.

Hello Grace!
Are you
having a
good time
"Down on the
Farm"?
F. I. C.

Old Witch House, Salem, Mass. Where victims of witchcraft were condemned 1692.

WITCH HOUSE, SALEM, MASS.   COPYRIGHT 1905, BY DETROIT PHOTOGRAPHIC CO.

MAIN ENTRANCE. OLD WITCH HOUSE. BUILT 1635. SALEM. MASS.

The Roger William's & Old Witch House, Salem, Mass.

Salem, Mass.
Roger Williams House or Witch House.
Ye Oldest House in Salem. Erected before 1635.

Salem, Mass., Witch House.

541. THE WITCH HOUSE BUILT IN 1634, SALEM, MASS.   1905 COPYRIGHT BY METROPOLITAN NEWS CO., BOSTON.

Salem, Mass., Witch House.

N & FRISBEE

G 6698 Roger Williams House or Old Witch House, built 1635, Salem, Mass.

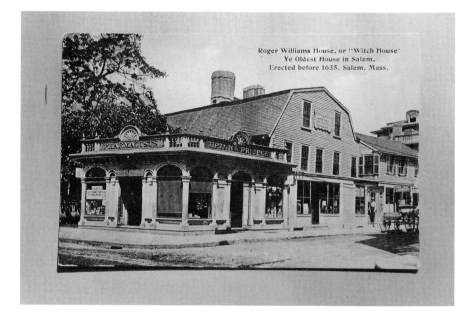

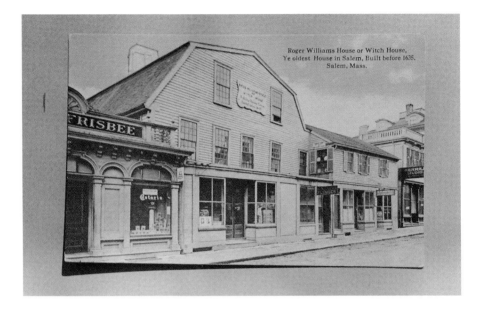

Roger Williams House or Witch House,
Ye oldest House in Salem, Built before 1635,
Salem, Mass.

Old Witch House, Built 1642, Salem, Mass.

Old Witch House, Built 1642, Salem, Mass.

Roger Williams House or Old Witch House, built 1635, Salem, Mass.

Ten views of Gallows Hill, which looks down onto the town. Here people came to watch the hangings. Some came out of curiosity, some as mourners, and some for entertainment. Here, after most people had gone home, the victims were cut down and some were tossed into unmarked graves so shallow that limbs and flesh still stuck up out of the ground. One can almost imagine, in this bleak and barren-looking place, the Reverend Burroughs with a noose around his neck reciting the Lord's Prayer and the people murmuring that the hangings should stop. One can also, imagine Cotton Mather sitting on his horse, telling the condemned to repent and hastening the executioners about their tasks. On September 22, eight people were hung at one time. It was the last execution and, perhaps because of the size of the execution and the piety of those who died, the outcry became so great that it had to be the last.

1301—Gallows Hill, Salem, Mass. Here the People were hanged for Witchcraft 1692.
I will try and call to see you the next time I am in Lawrence, remember me to your mother L. J. C.

Gallows Hill, where Witches were hanged.

Greetings from Salem, Mass.

Gallows Hill, where Witches were hanged.

Salem, Mass.

5400— Gallows Hill, Salem, Mass. Here the People were hanged for Witchcraft, 1692.

5400—Gallows Hill. Salem. Mass. Here the People were hanged for Witchcraft. 1692

Salem, Mass. Gallows Hill. The Ledges and Pond

1301—Gallows Hill, Salem, Mass.   Here the People were hanged for Witchcraft 1692.

I am having a good time

Gallows Hill—Salem.

BEVERLY

Which Witch is which? The image of the witch varies and changes over the years, but has never achieved the modern vamp image of Elvira. $7 to $15 each

THE SALEM WITCH. SALEM, MASS.

107738

The Salem Witch, Salem, Mass.

107738 N

Ye Salem Witch.

Ye Salem Witch, Salem, Mass.

THE DUCKING STOOL USED IN EARLY TIMES IN NEW ENGLAND

Jay. 11, 07

Well how do you like this weather? I got quite a ducking the other day but there weren't quite as many observers as there are here.

As ever your cousin Wm.

The ducking stool was an ingenious method of trying witches. If she drowned she was innocent, if she lived she was guilty. Either way she couldn't win. There is no record of ducking taking place in Salem, though it had been used in New England. $12.

Three mini postcards, small versions of the larger ones. $4 each.

Jail attic roof, 1684. The roof boards slope to the eaves, covered by a roof of 1764 vintage. No printer took credit for this card, but it makes one wonder why they thought the attic was so interesting. The contents maybe, but the attic of the jail? Why not the jail itself?

Two postcard folders showing the Salem witch and the Witch House. These multi-view postcard folders allowed people to get many views for less money. Because they don't frame or display well, they have a value well below what they should have. $4 each.

128

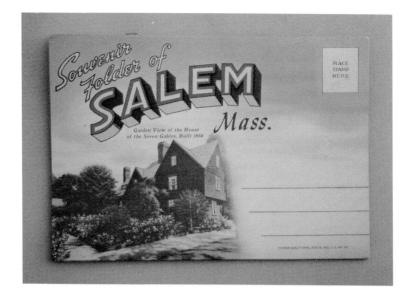

The back of a Salem folder which shows the House of Seven Gables on the front. $4.

One of the most interesting of all the postcards made shows the pandemonium of the trials. Notice the lack of space, the amount of people, and the chaos of motion that is taking place. George Jacobs' trial was very similar to those of his fellow victims. Imagine the fear of everyone pointing at you and saying you were the cause of their torment.

13270 "TRIAL OF GEORGE JACOBS OF SALEM FOR WITCHCRAFT", ESSEX INSTITUTE, SALEM, MASS.   COPR. DETROIT PUBLISHING CO.

Trial for Witchcraft of George Jacobs, who was hanged at Gallows Hill, Salem, Mass in 1692.

The old George Jacobs' house was in Old Salem Village, now known as Danvers. George Jacobs was another unfortunate victim of the witch hysteria. A few homes like these have survived and have been preserved. They are an important part of our national heritage.

Geo. Jacob's House. Occupant was hanged as a Witch, 1692.

Salem, Mass.

Postcards of the linen period were textured and you can see the paper texture quite clearly through the color of the printing. $6.

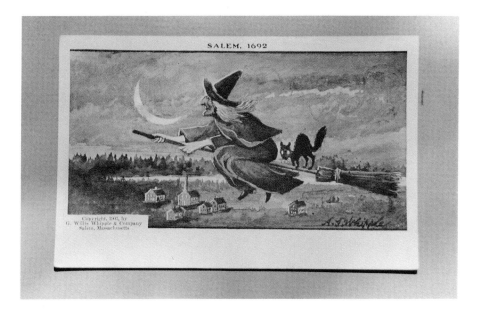

G. Willis Whipple & Co. produced this card, drawn by A. F. Whipple. This card, viewed under a magnifying glass, has such depth it appears three dimensional. $10.

Though there are no portraits of the female witches, it is hard to believe that even a composite looked like the image of the Salem Witch of the postcards. $8.

Variations of cards appear because of second, third, etc., printings, and because the same image was often printed by more than one printer. $8 each.

Three very different renditions of the same image. $8 each.

Howard was fortunate that Lena remembered him on her trip to Salem as this is a very scarce card showing the pins which were supposedly used by the witches to torment and torture the witnesses. $15.

Front and reverse. In 1878 many advertising trade cards were still printed in black and white. Dr Norman's foot salve could be purchased at Farrington & Luscomb Apothecaries. Obviously Mr. Farrington was so impressed with this miraculous corn salve that he produced an advertising card for it with a nice image of the Witch House, some information about it, and a press release for his drug store and new drug. A bit corny, even for 1878. $25.

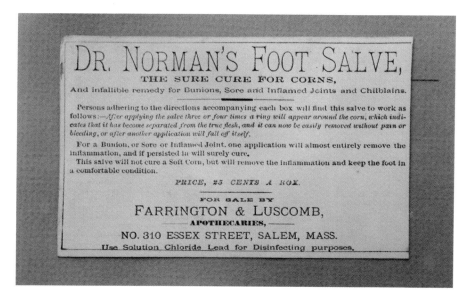

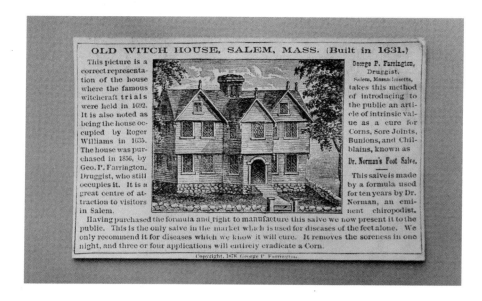

A rare advertising trade card issued by Daniel Low "Diamonds, Watches, Jewelry, and Silverware." It is surprising that they did not advertise their line of Witch City souvenirs. $15.

These four red witches look like the pen wipers that Daniel Low sold in their catalogue. $15.

"Bug-Rid, Skeeter-Rid, Rat-rid, Effective, Rid it does." An interesting claim by the Salem Chemical & Supply Co. in Salem. $10.

An interesting variation of the Salem witch as she and her cat have added an imp onto the back of their broom and, instead of a moon, they fly past a Jack O Lantern. $8.

Ye Salem Witches cause a traffic jam above the streets of Salem. A laughing moon and a solitary, fleeing pedestrian on the road below add a bit of humor to the card. $8.

W. B. Porter, copyright 1905. Poor old witch doesn't look like she's having much fun conjuring up these little hellions. $10.

W. B. Porter, 1905, companion card to the one on Page 141 showing an uncomfortably seated witch who doesn't seem very happy about her lofty position. $10.

The plate on this card might not come in the color printed on the card, but you will see it earlier in the book in fine china, in more than one size and color. $15.

Published by the Salem Press Co., this nicely laid-out card was given compliments of Dane Smith Co., which offered a healthy discount, though it neglected to tell us on what.

A cutsie, modern version of the witch. $2.

How the Witch House looks today. Modern chrome card. $1.

This is my favorite witch card. Dressed in orange with her black cat, this pleasant looking, elderly witch looks through a window into another era. $15.